A FIRST LOOK AT BATS

A FIRST LOOK AT SERIES

Each of the nature books in this series is planned to develop the child's powers of observation—to train him or her to notice distinguishing characteristics. A leaf is a leaf. A bird is a bird. An insect is an insect. That is true. But what makes an oak leaf different from a maple leaf? Why is a hawk different from an eagle or a beetle different from a bug?

Classification is a painstaking science. These books give a child the essence of the search for differences that is the basis for scientific classification.

LEAVES
FISH
MAMMALS
BIRDS
INSECTS
FROGS AND TOADS
SNAKES, LIZARDS, AND OTHER REPTILES
ANIMALS WITH BACKBONES
ANIMALS WITHOUT BACKBONES
FLOWERS
THE WORLD OF PLANTS
MONKEYS AND APES
SHARKS
WHALES
CATS
DOGS
HORSES
SEASHELLS
DINOSAURS
SPIDERS
ROCKS
BIRD NESTS
KANGAROOS, KOALAS, AND OTHER ANIMALS WITH POUCHES
OWLS, EAGLES, AND OTHER HUNTERS OF THE SKY
POISONOUS SNAKES
CATERPILLARS
SEALS, SEA LIONS, AND WALRUSES
ANIMALS WITH HORNS
ANIMALS THAT EAT OTHER ANIMALS
DUCKS, GEESE, AND SWANS

A FIRST LOOK AT BATS

Millicent E. Selsam and Joyce Hunt

Illustrations by Harriett Springer

WALKER AND COMPANY

NEW YORK

First published in the United States of America in 1991
by Walker Publishing Company, Inc.

Published simultaneously in Canada by Thomas Allen & Son
Canada, Limited, Markham, Ontario

Library of Congress Cataloging-in-Publication Data
Selsam, Millicent Ellis, 1912–
A first look at bats / Millicent E. Selsam and Joyce Hunt:
illustrations by Harriett Springer.
p.   cm.—(A First look at series)
Includes index.
Summary: Describes the distinctive characteristics of bats and
views several different species.
ISBN 0-8027-8135-7—ISBN 0-8027-8136-5 (reinforced)
1. Bats—Juvenile literature. [1. Bats.] I. Hunt, Joyce.
II. Springer, Harriett, ill. III. Title. IV. Series: Selsam,
Millicent Ellis, 1912– First look at series.
QL737.C5S45 1991
599.4—dc20   91-2862
CIP
AC

Printed in the United States of America
2 4 6 8 10 9 7 5 3 1

For Gideon

The authors wish to thank James Doherty, general curator of the New York Zoological Society, for reading the text of this book.

What is a bat?
A bat is an animal that flies.

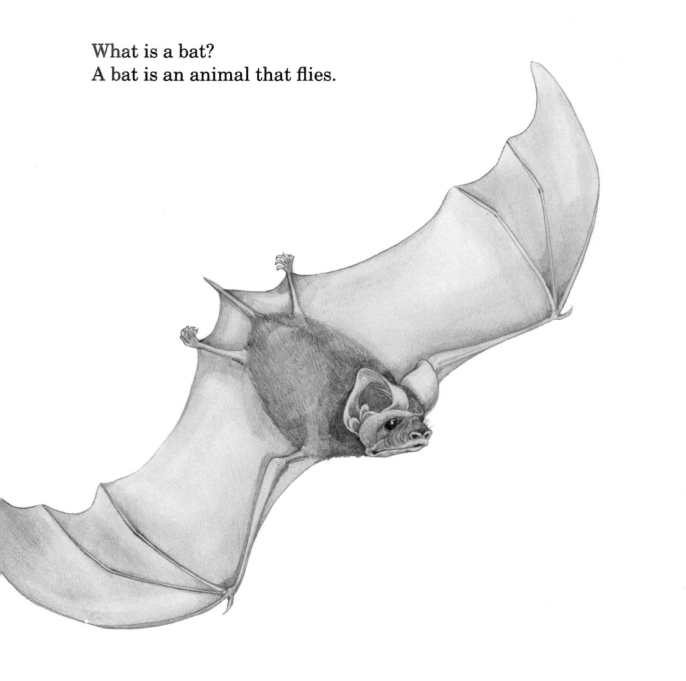

This animal flies.
Is it a bat?

No. It is a bird.
Birds have feathers.
Bats have fur.

Animals that have fur or hair are mammals.
Baby mammals nurse on their mother's milk.

Is this picture upside down? No.
Most bats hang with their heads down
while resting.

Bats are the only mammals that can fly.
They have wings.

Bats' wings are made of thin skin that is
stretched between their long fingers.
This skin is also attached to their
body and legs.

The small thumb is free and has a claw.

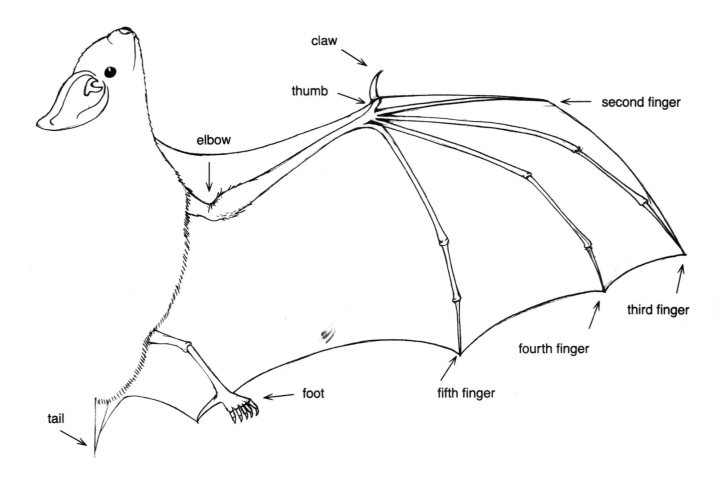

9

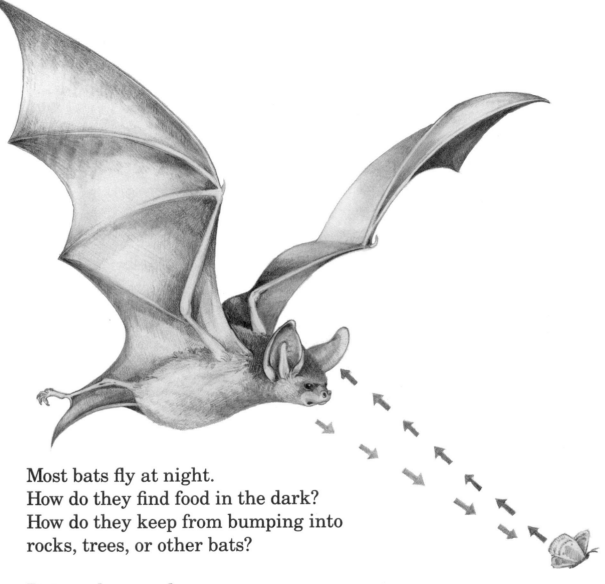

Most bats fly at night.
How do they find food in the dark?
How do they keep from bumping into
rocks, trees, or other bats?

Bats make sounds.
The sounds strike anything in their path
and bounce back as echos.
The echos help the bats locate (find)
where things are.
This is called *echolocation* (ek-oh-lo-KAY-shun).

During the day most bats rest in caves,
tree hollows, or the attics of houses.
Sometimes millions of bats rest together
in one place.

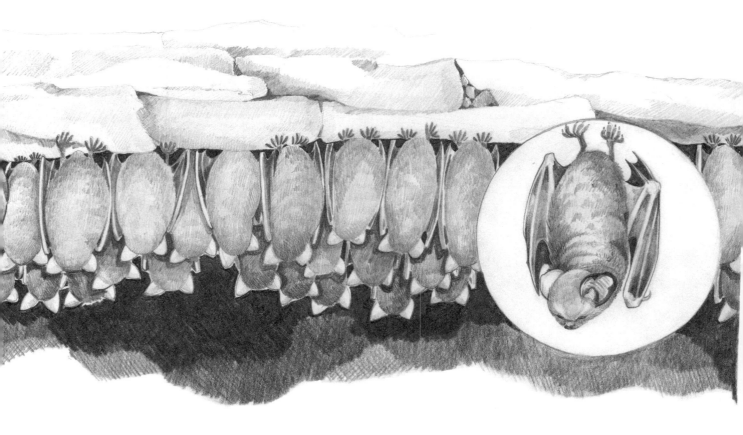

All bats do not look alike.
How do we tell them apart?
Some are big.
Some are small.
Some have tails.
Some do not.
Some have odd faces.
Some have odd noses or ears.

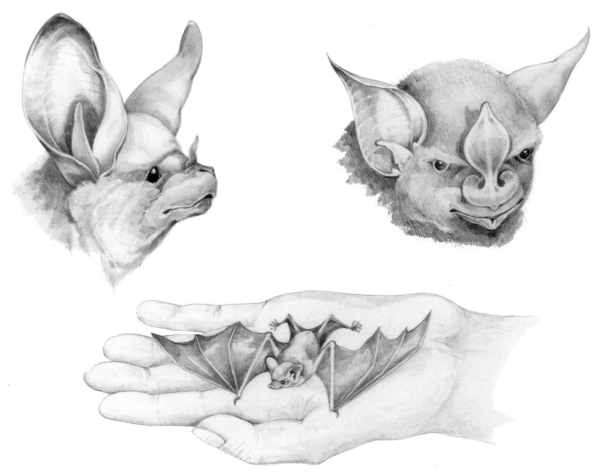

Look at this bat's nose.
The skin flap is called a *nose leaf*.
It helps the bat echolocate.

nose leaf

Commerson's Leaf-nosed Bat

The noses of these bats help tell them apart.

Match the bat to its name:

Tube-nosed Bat   Spear-nosed Bat

Look in this bat's ear.
This skin flap is called a *tragus* (*tray*—gus).
It helps the bat hear.

Eastern Pipistrelle

The ears of these bats help tell them apart.

Which bat has short round ears?
Which one has long rabbit-like ears?

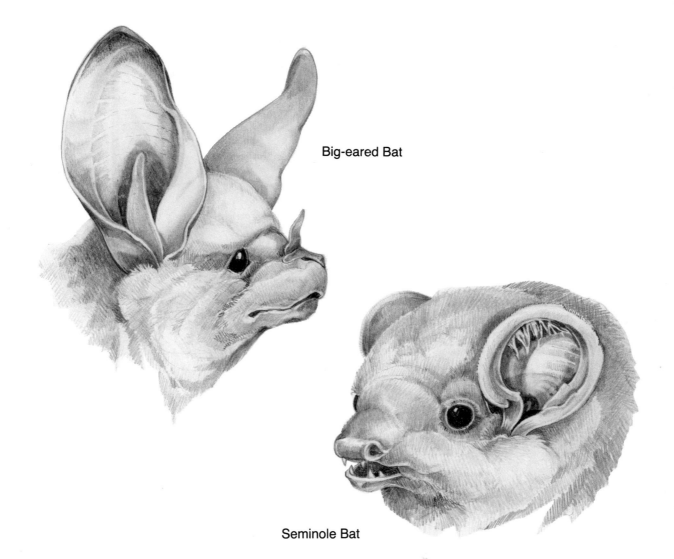

Big-eared Bat

Seminole Bat

Look at these faces!

Match these bats to their names:

Wrinkle-faced Bat   Slit-faced Bat   Hairless Bulldog Bat

19

You can tell some bats from others
because of their markings.

Which one has white spots on its back?
Which one is all white?

Sometimes the tails are a clue.

Look for the bat with no tail.
Look for the one with a long tail.

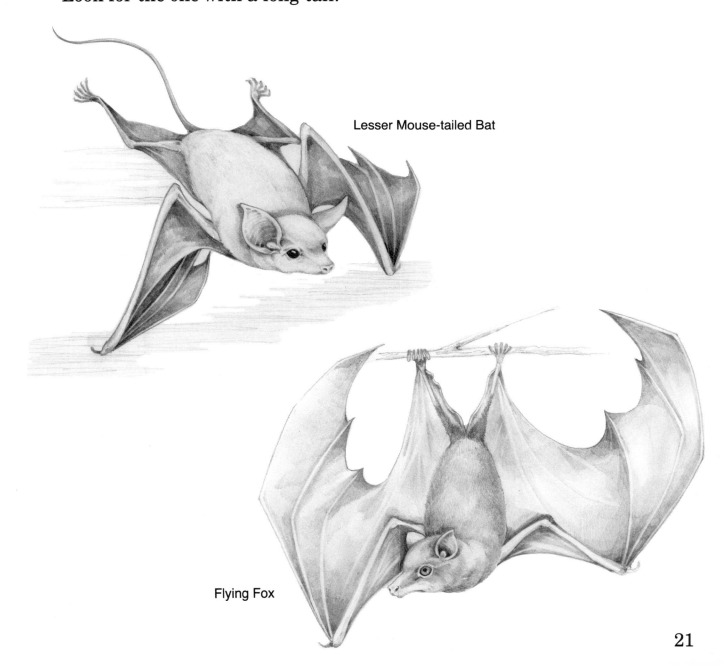

Lesser Mouse-tailed Bat

Flying Fox

This bat is called a Flying Fox.
Notice its large eyes.
Flying Foxes have good eyesight.
Most of them can find their way
without using echolocation.

Flying Foxes are the largest bats.

Here is the smallest bat.

Kitti's Hog-nosed Bat

This is a Vampire Bat.

On dark nights it hops silently to
where farm animals are sleeping.
It makes a small cut in the animal's
skin with its razor-sharp teeth and then
laps up the blood with its tongue.

It is the only mammal that eats nothing
but blood.

Most bats eat insects
or fruit.

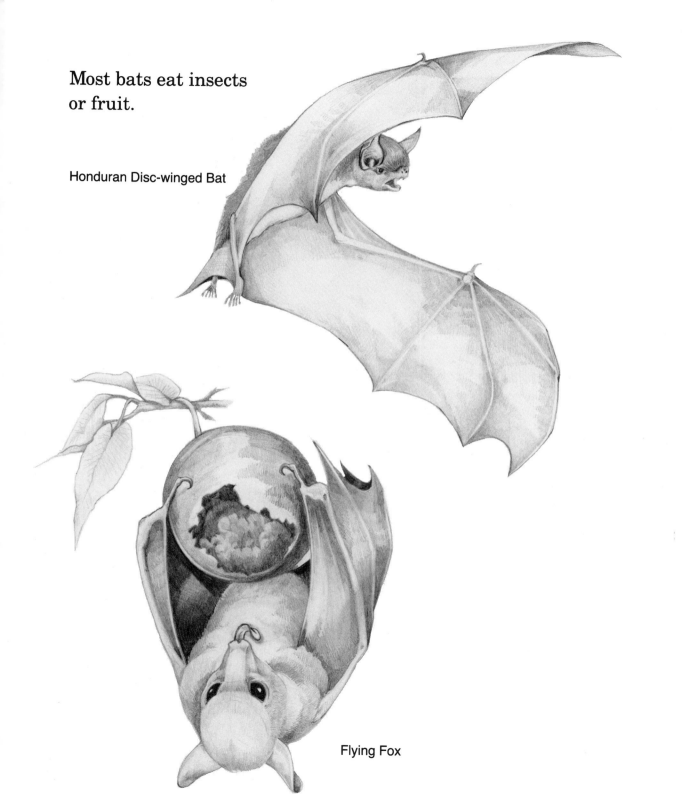

Honduran Disc-winged Bat

Flying Fox

25

Some eat flower nectar.

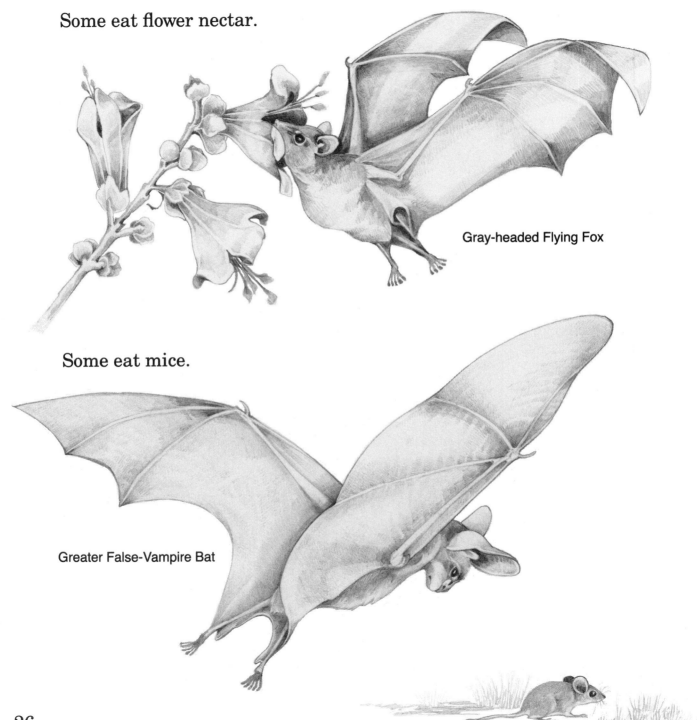

Gray-headed Flying Fox

Some eat mice.

Greater False-Vampire Bat

Many people are afraid of bats.
But bats do not hurt us.
They are useful.

Bats eat huge numbers of insects.

Bats that eat flower nectar carry pollen
from flower to flower.
Without these bats the plants would die out.

Bat waste, called *guano* (*gwan*-oh),
is used as fertilizer for plants.

Some gardeners put bat houses in their gardens
to attract bats that will eat harmful insects.

Bats should be protected.

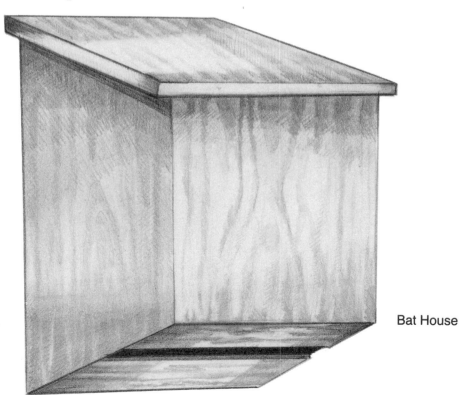

Bat House

Where bats are found:

NORTH AMERICA

Spotted Bat

Eastern Pipistrelle

Big-eared Bat

Caribbean White Bat

Vampire Bat

Honduran
Disc-winged Bat

Wrinkle-faced Bat

SOUTH AMERICA

Spear-nosed Bat

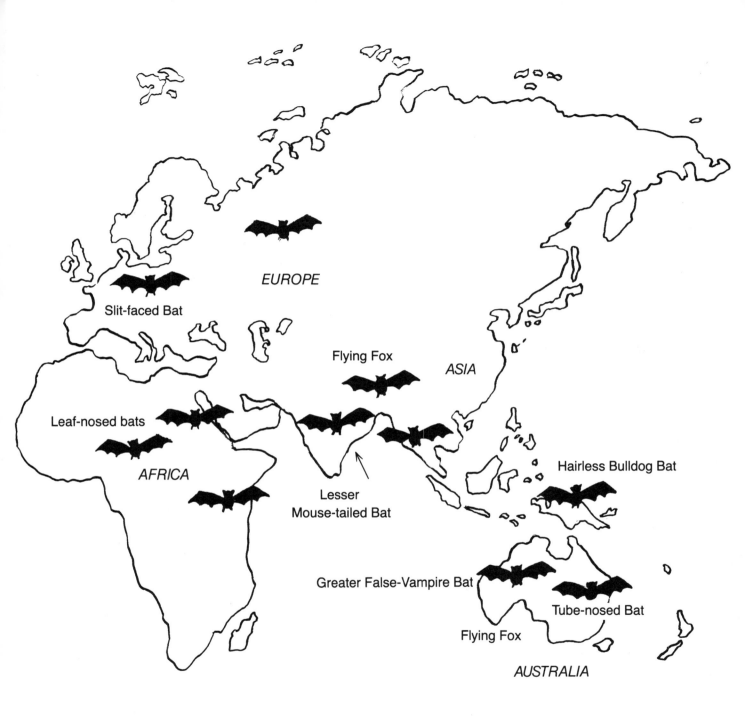

Slit-faced Bat

EUROPE

Flying Fox

ASIA

Leaf-nosed bats

AFRICA

Lesser
Mouse-tailed Bat

Hairless Bulldog Bat

Greater False-Vampire Bat

Tube-nosed Bat

Flying Fox

AUSTRALIA

29

To tell bats apart:

Look at their noses.

Look at their ears.

Look at their faces.

Look at their markings.

Look at their tails.

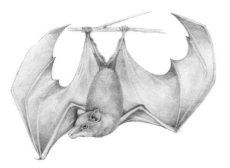

Look at their size.

Look at their teeth.

Bats in This Book